JA'MARR CHASE

BY CIARA O'NEAL

Apex is distributed by North Star Editions:
sales@northstareditions.com | 888-417-0195

Produced for Apex by Red Line Editorial.

Photographs ©: Aaron Doster/AP Images, cover, 4–5, 8–9, 18–19; Daniel Kucin Jr./AP Images, 1, 20; James Patterson/AP Images, 6–7; Shutterstock Images, 10–11, 12, 21, 22–23; Andy Altenburger/Icon Sportswire/AP Images, 13; Eric Gay/AP Images, 14–15; Gregory Payan/AP Images, 16–17; Ed Zurga/AP Images, 24; Jeff Dean/AP Images, 26–27, 29

Library of Congress Control Number: 2022922454

ISBN
978-1-63738-553-1 (hardcover)
978-1-63738-607-1 (paperback)
978-1-63738-711-5 (ebook pdf)
978-1-63738-661-3 (hosted ebook)

Printed in the United States of America
Mankato, MN
082023

NOTE TO PARENTS AND EDUCATORS

Apex books are designed to build literacy skills in striving readers. Exciting, high-interest content attracts and holds readers' attention. The text is carefully leveled to allow students to achieve success quickly. Additional features, such as bolded glossary words for difficult terms, help build comprehension.

TABLE OF CONTENTS

CHAPTER 1

KEY CATCH 4

CHAPTER 2

CHASING SUCCESS 10

CHAPTER 3

GOING PRO 16

CHAPTER 4

ON THE RISE 22

COMPREHENSION QUESTIONS • 28
GLOSSARY • 30
TO LEARN MORE • 31
ABOUT THE AUTHOR • 31
INDEX • 32

KEY CATCH

t's Week 17 of the 2021 season. The Cincinnati Bengals are tied with the Kansas City Chiefs in the fourth quarter. They just need a field goal to win.

The Cincinnati Bengals played the Kansas City Chiefs on January 2, 2022.

The Bengals' **quarterback** takes the snap. Ja'Marr Chase runs down the field. He looks over his shoulder and searches for a pass.

FAST FACT

Ja'Marr Chase plays wide receiver. He catches passes from the quarterback.

Ja'Marr Chase speeds past a Chiefs defender.

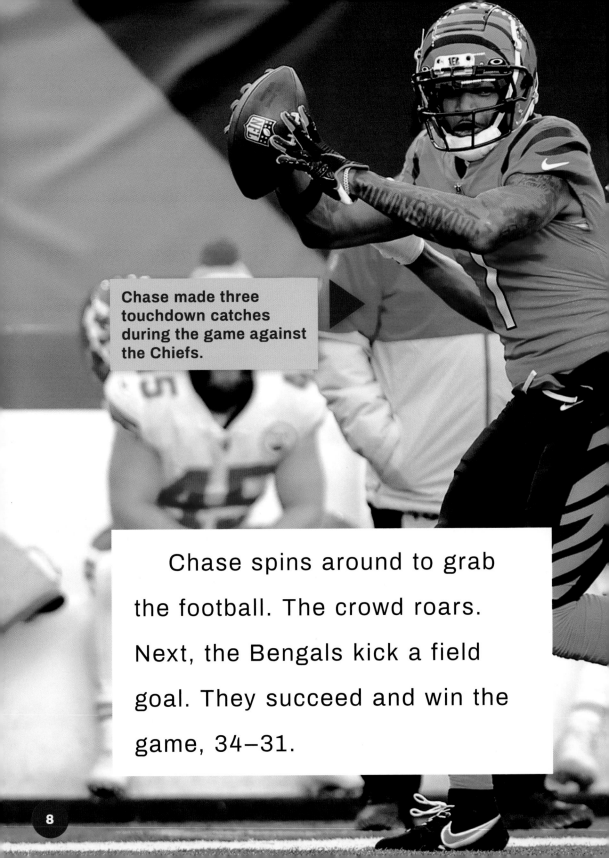

Chase made three touchdown catches during the game against the Chiefs.

Chase spins around to grab the football. The crowd roars. Next, the Bengals kick a field goal. They succeed and win the game, 34–31.

ROOKIE RECORD

Chase's catch broke a record. He had 266 **receiving yards** in the game. That was the most ever for an NFL **rookie** in a single game.

CHAPTER 2

CHASING SUCCESS

Ja'Marr Chase grew up near New Orleans, Louisiana. He played several sports in high school. But football was his favorite. And he was very good at it.

New Orleans is the largest city in Louisiana.

LSU plays at Tiger Stadium in Baton Rouge, Louisiana.

Colleges all over the country wanted Ja'Marr to play for them. But he decided to stay close to home. He chose Louisiana State University (LSU).

ALL-STAR ATHLETE

Besides football, Ja'Marr competed in basketball and track in high school. He excelled at all three sports. In 2017, he was the best long jumper in the state.

Ja'Marr Chase (1) joined future NFL receiver Justin Jefferson (2) at LSU.

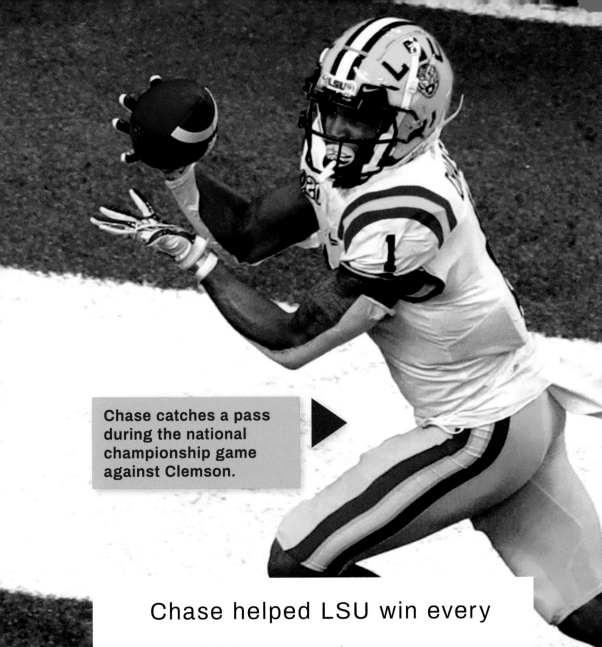

Chase catches a pass during the national championship game against Clemson.

Chase helped LSU win every game of his second season. His team also won the college football **championship** that year.

CHAPTER 3

GOING PRO

Chase left LSU after his second season. He wanted to prepare for the 2021 NFL **Draft**. This choice paid off. The Cincinnati Bengals chose him in the first round.

Chase was the fifth pick in the 2021 NFL Draft.

Chase had more than 100 receiving yards and scored a touchdown during his first NFL game.

Chase quickly found success in the NFL. He became the youngest player to catch four touchdown passes in his first three games.

FAST FACT

Chase caught a total of 13 touchdowns in his rookie season.

Chase sprints toward the end zone during a game against the Baltimore Ravens.

Chase often teamed up with quarterback Joe Burrow. Chase could run fast to get open. And Burrow had great aim. Together, they made many big plays.

A GREAT DUO

Chase and Burrow met in college. Both played football for LSU. There, Burrow threw to Chase for 23 touchdowns. The two players also became close friends.

Joe Burrow won the Heisman Trophy in 2019. This award goes to the best college player each year.

CHAPTER 4

ON THE RISE

Chase led the Bengals to the **playoffs** his rookie year. They won their **division** for the first time since 2015.

The Bengals are part of the AFC North division. Their home stadium is in Cincinnati, Ohio.

The Bengals went on to play in the AFC Championship. They were down by 18 points. But Chase didn't give up. He helped his team win in overtime.

FAST FACT

The Bengals also won the AFC Championship in 1981 and 1988.

Chase had six catches and scored a touchdown during the AFC Championship Game.

The Bengals went on to the Super Bowl. They lost a close game against the Los Angeles Rams. Even so, fans were excited. They looked forward to more great seasons from their new star.

AWARD WINNER

Chase was named the 2021 **Offensive** Rookie of the Year. He had 1,455 receiving yards. That was the most ever for a rookie.

Chase had an average of 85.6 receiving yards per game during the 2021 season.

COMPREHENSION
QUESTIONS

Write your answers on a separate piece of paper.

1. Write a few sentences describing the main ideas of Chapter 4.

2. Would you rather be a quarterback like Joe Burrow or a wide receiver like Ja'Marr Chase? Why?

3. When did Chase and Burrow first become teammates?

    A. in high school
    B. in college
    C. in the NFL

4. Why would running fast be important for a wide receiver?

    A. Wide receivers need to get past defenders.
    B. Wide receivers need to tackle quarterbacks.
    C. Wide receivers need to kick field goals.

5. What does **excelled** mean in this book?

*Besides football, Ja'Marr competed in basketball and track in high school. He **excelled** at all three sports.*

    A. did not like

    B. did not play

    C. was very good

6. What does **excited** mean in this book?

*Even so, fans were **excited**. They looked forward to more great seasons from their new star.*

    A. happy about what might happen

    B. afraid of what might happen

    C. thinking about the past

Answer key on page 32.

GLOSSARY

championship
The final game that decides the winner of a tournament.

division
A group of teams within a league.

draft
A system where professional teams choose new players.

offensive
Related to the team or players who are trying to score.

playoffs
A set of games played after the regular season to decide which team will be the champion.

quarterback
A player who directs the offense and throws the ball.

receiving yards
The number of yards gained by a receiver on a passing play.

rookie
A player in their first year.

TO LEARN MORE

BOOKS

Coleman, Ted. *Cincinnati Bengals All-Time Greats*. Mendota
   Heights, MN: Press Box Books, 2022.

Meier, William. *Cincinnati Bengals*. Minneapolis: Abdo
   Publishing, 2020.

Mitchell, Bo. *The Super Bowl*. Mendota Heights, MN: Apex
   Editions, 2023.

ONLINE RESOURCES

Visit **www.apexeditions.com** to find links and resources
related to this title.

ABOUT THE AUTHOR

Ciara O'Neal is an author of many books and a mother of
many children. This one is for Isaac, who never gives up.

INDEX

B
Burrow, Joe, 20–21

C
Cincinnati Bengals, 4, 6, 8, 16, 22, 25–26

K
Kansas City Chiefs, 4

L
Los Angeles Rams, 26
Louisiana State University (LSU), 12, 15, 16, 21

N
New Orleans, Louisiana, 10
NFL, 9, 16, 19

P
playoffs, 22

Q
quarterback, 6, 20

R
rookie, 9, 19, 22, 26

S
Super Bowl, 26

T
touchdown, 15, 19, 21

W
wide receiver, 6

ANSWER KEY:
1. Answers will vary; 2. Answers will vary; 3. B; 4. A; 5. C; 6. A